Blue Marble, L.L.C. 205 Brazos Street Austin, TX 78701 1/800-860-9442
www.bluemarblemusic.com email: info@bluemarblemusic.com

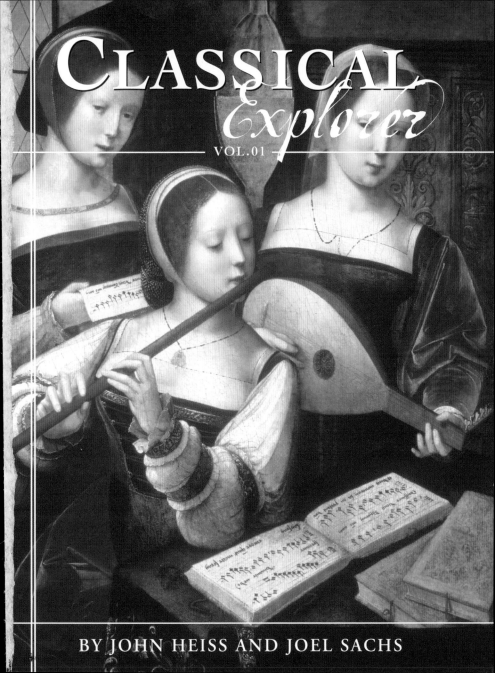

CLASSICAL
Explorer
VOL.01

BY JOHN HEISS AND JOEL SACHS

Founder's Invitation

What you hold in your hands is the result of exposing my total ignorance of classical music to two of the world's best teachers. The genius and unending passion of John Heiss and Joel Sachs transformed my curiosity into an inspiring discovery of one of the world's great art forms. The big surprises for me were Palestrina, Haydn, Berlioz and Sousa – how could all this music be readily available, yet lie beyond so many hurdles that made it undiscoverable?

With confidence that the generosity and knowledge of Heiss and Sachs may do the same for you, I extend an invitation to you to embrace your own curiosity and use Blue Marble's Classical Explorer to leap-frog the hurdles that are usually present when exploring classical music. May the music you hear and the discoveries you make enrich your life. That is our goal at Blue Marble Music.

Steve Stone, Founder
Blue Marble Music

P.S. The painting at left is of a place I have walked past several times with little more than an impression. After discovering the role of this sacred place in the history of western music (in the pages on Gabrieli, Monteverdi and Schütz), I now find myself wanting to rush off to Venice to sit in the balconies of St. Mark's Basilica and soak up the view from where it all happened 400 years ago.

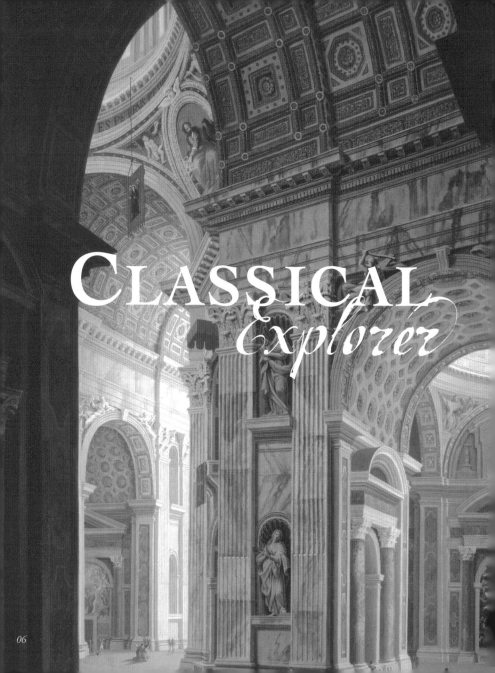

CLASSICAL
Explorer

OUTLINE

THE EXPERTS

JOHN HEISS

In 1967, John Heiss was recruited by the distinguished contemporary composer Gunther Schuller to teach music composition and history at New England Conservatory of Music in Boston. It did not take long for Heiss to become a favorite teacher of the students at NEC. Some 30 years later, Heiss' reputation has extended well beyond the students at NEC to the world's leading contemporary composers like Ligeti, Lutoslawski, Berio, Carter, Messiaen, Schuller, and Tippett, who regularly visit NEC at Heiss' invitation.

As an active composer, conductor and flutist, Heiss' works have been performed worldwide, and he has received awards and commissions from such renowned groups as the Rockefeller Foundation, the Guggenheim Foundation, National Endowment for the Arts and others.

A highlight of Heiss' early career was receiving the title of "pitch doctor" straight from Stravinsky himself after Heiss assisted a production of Stravinsky's work. Heiss has been principal flute of Boston Musica Viva and has performed with many local ensembles, including the Boston Symphony Orchestra.

Heiss received his B.A. in mathematics from Lehigh University and M.F.A. from Princeton University. His works are principally published by Boosey & Hawkes, E.C. Schirmer, and Elkus & Son.

JOEL SACHS

Joel Sachs joined the faculty of The Juilliard School in 1970 as a historian, and was the first chairman of its music history department. His activities soon extended beyond the historical. As founder-conductor of the New Juilliard Ensemble, a chamber orchestra for new music, he has commissioned many composers worldwide, and brought the ensemble to Germany, Israel, Poland, and Russia. He also directs Juilliard's annual FOCUS! Festival, and the Summergarden festival at New York's Museum of Modern Art, a cooperative project with Juilliard.

Following his first love and acclaimed talent, Sachs has performed a vast range of traditional and new music as both conductor and pianist. As co-director of the new-music ensemble Continuum, he has toured the group throughout the world.

Sachs has written extensively on 19th-century music history, and currently is preparing a biography of American composer Henry Cowell. He received his B.A. at Harvard and his M.A. and Ph.D. at Columbia.

MEDIEVAL PERIOD

THE BEGINNING

In the beginning there was music. Unfortunately, no one wrote it down. So we have no record of music that was composed before about 600 A.D. – when it is said that Pope Gregory sent out an edict to all churches requesting that they notate the music being sung during their services so the music would carry on to future generations (hence the term 'Gregorian Chant').

Many scholars believe notation of music was one of its most important innovations. If a notation system had not been developed, whole centuries of music would have been lost. Our view of music from this time is akin to looking through a telescope: We see a few amazing things and miss a few million.

MEDIEVAL STYLES

Imagine the passing of hundreds of years with music that has only one flowing melody and no background. The only documented music of the early Medieval period is *monophonic* (defined in glossary) vocal music performed in the church. Monophonic means music of one melodic line. There was only one melody, sung without instruments or accompaniment of any kind.

The radical 12th century technique that began to layer multiple melodies is called *polyphony* (pronounced pol.i'.funny). The song *Row, Row, Row Your Boat* (when sung by a group) is a perfect example of polyphony. Together with music notation, polyphony is considered by many scholars to be the most important achievement of western music's development, and it remains a central feature of western music today.

Gregorian Chant

This is where it all came from. You're going to hear something spare and ancient here, yet stunning in its simplicity. We'll get to the music you may be more familiar with soon enough, but there are a few discoveries worth making along the way. After a deep submersion in later music, it is refreshing to come back to the spiritual clarity of male voices all singing a single melody in unison in Latin.

Beata Dei Genetrix (Maria) "Blessed Be the Mother of God" (after 604)

This chant is a reverent meditation on the purity of the Virgin Mary and was usually sung during the holiday vespers.

Other Recommended Works: Any quality recording of Gregorian Chants

Hildegard Von Bingen (1098 - 1179)

Hildegard Von Bingen's work is the first we can connect to the name of a specific composer. What a treat it is to learn that a woman was leading the way in what many thought was a male-only field. She had the foresight to bind her compositions and preserve them, and we are now listening to a recording of one of her compositions almost 900 years later. The church practice required all-male choirs, but Hildegard wrote for the nuns of the convent she directed.

Studium Divinitatis, "Zeal for the Divine" (1140)

Listen closely and you'll hear the use of small melodic units that hint of the multi-voiced, multiple-melody music that appears later during the Renaissance. In this way, Hildegard provides a bridge for us between the Medieval and Renaissance eras.

ARS NOVA

In the early 1300's, there was another big shift in music called the Ars Nova – meaning "new art." This is the time when polyphony took off and music became far more complex in texture, and a new level of **dissonance** was introduced. This, together with rhythmic freedom, made the individual melodies more audible.

Significant Composers not included:
Machaut, Landini

The Voices

Soprano – High Voice of Child or Female

Alto – Low Voice of Child or Female

Counter Tenor – Very High Male Voice

Tenor – High Male Voice

Bass – Low Male Voice

RENAISSANCE PERIOD

In the early 1400's, the music Gods stood up and pronounced: "It is now time to experiment with more emotion in music." Actually, we don't know for sure if they pronounced it or if it just happened.

❖

Emotion wasn't the only new element creeping into music in the late Renaissance; there were hints of *chords* and the *major scale* as well, although they weren't named yet (but you can hear them!). Although the choir was the major form of performance, instruments were just beginning to play an increasing role in music.

The big technical leap forward in the Renaissance was the development of *imitative* layering of polyphonic melodies. This technique allowed composers to extend a few pithy melodic ideas into complex, large-scale compositions. To appreciate the importance of imitative layering, it is helpful to know that this technique has been the central focus of composition for the 500-plus years since its invention.

Significant Composers not included:
Byrd, di Lasso, Farmer, Marenzio, Morley, Tallis

Josquin Desprez (1450 - 1521)

Almost unanimously considered the greatest composer of the Renaissance, Josquin was the master of complex polyphonic harmony and composer of the era's most elaborate sacred and secular music. The works of Josquin show the development and perfection of multi-voiced melody and richly textured vocal compositions.

Missa L'homme Arme sexti toni – Kyrie mvt. (circa 1500)

This complex setting of *Kyrie Eleison* ("Lord have mercy") is the first movement of a mass that integrates melodic fragments of the **secular** tune "The Armed Man." Written for both male and female voices, this Kyrie (pronounced ker´.e.ay) features four intertwining voices in a prayer of penance, divine redemption, and moral strength.

*Other Recommended Works: Any other mass; numerous **motets** and secular vocal music. Any recording of the Tallis Scholars on Gimell Records.*

Giovanni Pierluigi da Palestrina (1525 - 1594)

Here it is! The *major scale* as we know it today is finally beginning to make its first appearance. It doesn't have a name yet, but Palestrina's work is filled with the sounds of the chords in the major scale. Though similar to Josquin, Palestrina's works represent a cross-section of the old Renaissance polyphony and the new pre-Baroque chord-based musical structure. Palestrina's illustrious career culminated in his being named the choir master of the Giuilian Chapel at St. Peter's Basilica in Rome. Altogether, he composed more than 100 masses, vast amounts of other sacred music, and even secular vocal pieces.

Missa Papae Marcelli – Gloria mvt. (1567)

This elegant "Gloria" movement is from a celebratory mass for Marcellus, the new pope who proposed a radical simplification of church music in the wake of the Protestant Reformation. Palestrina presented his *Missa Papae Marcelli* (Mass for Pope Marcellus) at the pope's coronation, and its purity, clarity and power helped avert a return to monophonic plainchant in Catholic services.

Other Recommended Works: Any recordings of Palestrina by the Tallis Scholars on Gimell Records.

❖

BAROQUE PERIOD

On January 1st in 1600, church bells rang all across Europe, and they said: "It's here! A new era!". Well it actually took twenty years or so for that to happen, but on a historical scale, that is an amazingly rapid shift.

If there was a central voice of composers of the early Baroque, it would have said: "There are too many overlapping melodies that get in the way of the words. Let's get down to a fundamental single line, with words that we can understand, and then design the rest of the composition to make that top melody and it's underlying bass-line come through loud and clear. *And with emotion!*" This is a simple way of explaining *two-voice polarity* (another technique that is found in almost everything we hear on the radio today).

The idea to set an entire emotional stage play to music sprang up in Florence. This new form, soon called *opera*, quickly spread across Europe. Later Baroque composers restricted themselves to exploring only one emotion within each piece. This is called the *single affect* doctrine.

Significant Composers not included: Scarlatti and Vivaldi

Giovanni Gabrieli (1553 - 1612)

Here come the instruments! Working in then-powerful and rebellious Venice, Giovanni Gabrieli was Europe's first major instrumental composer and first significant figure of Baroque music. As organist and resident composer at the innovative St. Mark's Basilica, Gabrieli experimented with lavish productions featuring brass accompaniment, multiple choirs and dramatic organ flourishes.

St. Mark's Basilica

Sacrae Symphoniae, Book 1: Canzon Septimi Toni a 8, no. 2 (1597)

There's more than one brass ensemble here. Gabrieli put choirs and brass ensembles in balconies opposite each other and wrote music so that tones from each would meet in the middle, creating combinations of notes that neither group actually performed. How's that for original? In this piece, one brass ensemble is echoing a second. The upbeat, exuberant music is written exclusively for instruments rather than voices, representing one of the first large scale works composed without an accompanying text.

Claudio Monteverdi (1567 - 1643)

St. Mark's Basilica in Venice was a 'happening' place around 1600. Monteverdi, as a student of Gabrieli, followed in his footsteps as head of music at St. Mark's. Monteverdi embodied the musical transition from Renaissance to Baroque, and rapidly took the idea of opera from experiment to great art. A prolific composer in vocal, chamber, instrumental, orchestral and opera, he was equally at home in sacred and secular contexts. Monteverdi embraced complex human emotions in his madrigals – dealing with love, war, and other earthly endeavors.

A Un Giro Sol de Begl'occhi ("At But One Glance") from Book of Madrigals: IV (1603)

Here is Monteverdi's groundbreaking use of **dissonance** to express pain. In this case, it is the pain of rejection felt by a spurned lover ("You hurt me so bad that I die…"). About midway through the piece, you'll hear it – a seeming 'wrong note' that creates a jarring tension and a new expression of human emotion in Baroque composition. "Music is going to the dogs!," his critics attacked. Monteverdi let them know that there was a new practice and a new era coming in music that would allow the expression of human emotions other than happiness.

Other Recommended Works: Operas:
"L'incoronazione di Poppea"; "Orfeo"

Heinrich Schütz (1585 - 1672)

Schütz had the unique advantage of studying in Italy under Gabrieli and as a contemporary of Monteverdi (the two greatest composers of his time). This no doubt gave him quite a repertoire when he traveled back to Germany and applied his new techniques to native Lutheran texts. This musical cross-pollination had a profound, lasting effect on German and Austrian music forever after. The richest single vein of music to ever come from one part of the world is rounding the corner of history soon. Think of it – the run of Bach, Handel, Haydn, Mozart, Schubert, Mendelssohn, Schumann, Brahms, Wagner and Schoenberg all arose from Schütz's study in Italy.

Die Himmel Erzahlen Die Ehre Gottes ("The Heavens Foretell the Glory of God") from Geistliche Chormusik ("Sacred Choral Music") (1648)

Although "The Heavens Foretell the Glory of God" is a late work of Schütz, it is written in a late Renaissance style and sounds as if we have slipped back in time after the Monteverdi piece. We picked it because it is a beautiful motet in six-part harmony.

Other Recommended Works: Sacred Symphonies Part III

George Frideric Handel (1685 - 1759)

Like wine, there are good years for musicians, and '85 was a good year. Both Bach and Handel were born. Handel ventured to Italy from Germany (like Schütz), where he learned the Italian melodic tradition and added it to the German polyphonic tradition. Handel is sometimes described as the 'Josquin' of his time – meaning (like Josquin Desprez) he was prolific at every form that was present in his time.

George Frideric Handel

Messiah: HWV 56: Hallelujah! Chorus
(circa 1743)

We are getting into the import and export of music with Handel's Messiah. Handel took the influences of Italy and Germany and went to England, where he wrote many works of great appeal to the British middle class. Tracing the path, we go from Italy to Germany to England. And now almost 300 years later, we have the powerful "Hallelujah!" chorus of *Messiah* as a Christmas musical standby familiar to many nations all over the world. International appeal – that was the essence of Handel.

Other Recommended Works: Israel in Egypt (oratorio); Any concerto of Handel

JOHANN SEBASTIAN BACH

Bach might just be the epicenter of classical music. For many scholars and lovers of Western music, Johann Sebastian Bach is the pivotal figure and greatest composer of the classical tradition – the proverbial Shakespeare of music. Unlike Handel, who enjoyed great fame in his lifetime, Bach was relatively unknown as a composer during his own lifetime. But in the early 19th century, musicians and audiences rediscovered the glories within Bach's compositions. With his rich harmonic *counterpoint*, he elevated western music to new heights.

One story is told that Bach heard that Vivaldi was visiting a town 120 miles away, so he walked over, copied Vivaldi's music down, heard the performances and then walked home to study the music. There is a point here more important than Bach's passion: travel now enabled composers to learn from their predecessors and contemporaries from other regions of the world. This new ability was as important as notation and polyphony in the development of western music.

CD 1 – Track 9

"Air" from Suite for Orchestra No. 3 in D major, BWV 1068 (1731)

There are four simultaneous melodic lines in this song-like movement which forms one section of a large *Suite* (set of dances). Upon repeated listening, the listener should try to focus on each line separately, since even the lines that seem to be *accompaniment* are beautiful on their own. In this work, Bach is effectively marrying the 'new' rhythms of Monteverdi with the 'eternal line' of Gregorian chant.

CD 1 – Track 10

Christmas Oratorio, BWV 248, Part One: "Triumph, Rejoicing",
(Opening Chorus) (1735)

Bach's "Christmas Oratorio" is actually a collection of *cantatas* that commemorate the glory of the holiday season. The lively percussion and powerful vocals show Bach at his most celebratory and joyous. Listen to the way Bach makes everything important, not just the tune. Listen to the way the instruments reinforce the feeling communicated by the words.

Other Recommended Works: Goldberg Variations (Glenn Gould); Cantata 140 ("Sleepers Awake!"); Cantata 105, St. Matthew Passion

> *"Aha! Here is something from which one can still learn!"*
>
> – Mozart (paraphrased), upon hearing his first Bach work.

CLASSIC PERIOD

Once again, young composers rebelled against the complexity of the highly ornamental late Baroque works. They forced music back to a simpler style – with emphasis on striking chords and keeping things clear – so the primary emotional message could come across with power.

The vogue for comic opera may have been as responsible for the change of styles as any rebellion or revolution. Comic opera required a style capable of quick and powerful dramatic contrasts. Moods and emotions stopped on a dime in opera, and then blasted off in a new direction. The *single-affect* style of the Baroque was incapable of dealing with this new demand and so a new style developed, from evolution more than revolution.

The symphony and opera as we know them today were now being used to tell dramatic human stories on a large stage. The stories grew longer; the audience grew broader; the venues grew into concert halls and arenas; and the depth and size of the music and instrumentation grew to fill the new space and medium. Music had entered the world of serious art and entertainment in a new way.

Franz Joseph Haydn

"Papa Haydn" is what friends and admirers called him. What a wonderful human being; he was the guy next door. Kind, happy, earthy. Sophisticated, yet approachable and loved by the common man. As the man goes, so goes his music – straightforward brilliance.

Haydn made the symphony what it is today. During the 18th century, he composed 104 them. This played a critical role in influencing Beethoven's choice to make the symphony his primary form. Continuing to compose well into his later years, Haydn wrote many of his most exuberant and energetic works in his seventies.

CD 1 – Track 11
Symphony No. 103, mvt. 4 (1795)

The structure of the movement can clearly be heard: it consists of a series of large sections each of which is introduced by a fanfare played by two French horns (as in the very beginning, where it is played twice in a row). Listen to the short idea that follows the first fanfares – it begins with four repeated notes, then a rapid descent and ascent – all in merely twelve notes. This little musical idea generates virtually everything that happens in the movement – a remarkable economy of means.

Other Recommended Works: Symphonies 88-104; Symphony No. 6; and String Quartets

Wolfgang Amadeus Mozart

As a mind-boggling child prodigy, Mozart began composing early: His first symphony at age six; his first opera at eleven. He diligently studied the music of his day and established himself as a master of every existing musical medium before the age of 30. Mozart's unique genius came in his ability to appeal to the lay listener *and* simultaneously please the connoisseurs with infinite and bottomless depth.

Haydn's influence brought depth to Mozart's early music. The two eventually became friends, and as Mozart matured into his late twenties and early thirties, it was Mozart that began influencing Haydn.

"Before God and as an honest man, I tell you that your son is the greatest composer known to me, in person or by name. He has taste, and what is more, the greatest knowledge of composition." – Joseph Haydn (age 53) speaking to Mozart's father about Mozart (age 29).

When Haydn was in his sixties, he received a commission to go to London. Mozart saw him off and reportedly cried, saying: "You are too old to take such a hazardous journey. I fear for what will happen to you." Haydn replied, "Don't worry, I have a lot of life left in me. We'll see each other again." As fate would have it, Mozart died at age 35, (after composing 600 major works) before Haydn's return.

CD 1 – TRACK 12
Don Giovanni, No. 7 Duettino, La ci darem la mano (1787)

This duet from the opera *Don Giovanni* is a nice example of Mozart's ability to infuse life into opera characters. In this scene, Don Giovanni is beginning to assert his traditional but despicable right to sleep with a peasant woman (Zerlina) before she marries. He prefers to seduce her rather than force the issue. She seems all too intrigued by him … and in the end (as the music accelerates) the lovers say, "Andiam …" ("I will …"). But she soon manages to avoid that fate.

CD 1 – TRACK 13
Die Zauberflote ("The Magic Flute") K 620: Overture (1791)

This spirited overture opens a work that many consider Mozart's signature piece. Certainly one of his most famous operas, *The Magic Flute (Die Zauberflöte)* conjures moods of mystery and optimism, and Mozart's embodiment of divine comedy.

CD 1 – TRACK 14
Piano Concerto No. 23 in A, K488, mvt. 2 (1786)

Piano Concerto No. 23 spends most of its time in the bright key of A major. But this movement, written in a reflective F# minor (the # signifies 'sharp'), provides a parenthetical sadness in the middle of the concerto. The overall architecture of the movement is in three sections; the second contrasts with the first; and the third is a varied restatement of the first.

Other Recommended Works: Symphony No.40; The Marriage of Figaro

LUDWIG VAN BEETHOVEN

This was a man of immense courage. A "Lion", he is sometimes called today. It was Beethoven's courage, as much as his musical genius that stretched all the norms of music into a gigantic new dimension, including length, range of contrasts and emotional states.

When Beethoven was in his early thirties, his hearing began a progressive deterioration that left him quite deaf and no longer able to function in his main breadwinning capacity as a piano virtuoso. However, the loss of hearing seems to have helped him pass beyond the conventionalities of the music of his time and to reach deeply into his imagination. His no-nonsense, bold and buoyant style ushered in the Romantic period.

CD 2 – TRACK 1

Symphony No. 3 in E flat major, op. 55; Allegro con brio (first mvt.)
(a.k.a. the 'Eroica' Symphony) (1803)

What a simple, almost trivial little motif he has here. And then he makes the most magnificent theme and development in all of music out of this simpleness. The 'Eroica' (Heroic) Symphony is considered his signature piece. Listen for the dissonance introduced just before the 2'30" mark, and compare the six beats of this note to Stravinsky's Rite of Spring on track 8 of CD 2. Listen also for how the little melodic fragment that follows the two loud chords at the opening finally becomes a real melody only in the last few minutes of the movement.

Other Recommended Works: Symphony No. 1; "Moonlight" Sonata (Piano Sonata Op. 27 No. 2); String Quartet op. 131; Symphony No. 9

ROMANTIC PERIOD

Beethoven was history's first 'rock star'. He was no longer alive after 1827, though you wouldn't know it. His daring and brilliance transformed the composer from servant to master. The composer was now king! If not for Beethoven, we might still view musicians as servants – and thus 'rock stars' might not exist.

◎

The personality of the composer was now becoming the dominant force in music, and by the 1840s music is coming from the inner emotional 'genius' – and it seems unlimited now in rhythm, form and harmony.

The whole music world is different now as well. Brilliant composers are no longer isolated across parts of Europe. There had been a foundation of learning and influence in place in Italy, Germany, France and England. As a result, musical cultures were now exploding across many nations.

Significant Composers not included: Schubert, Schumann, Wagner, Verdi and Tchaikowsky

FREDERIC CHOPIN

Chopin's work redefined the piano for 100 years. His precisionist and perfectionist style unearthed new colors of sound from the piano, giving it a new kind of expressiveness. He also showed remarkable imagination in taking popular styles (especially dances such as mazurkas, waltzes, and polonaises) and giving them a depth and variety that keeps them fresh and alive even now.

CD 2 – TRACK 2
Barcarolle for Piano in F sharp major, B 158, Op. 60 (1845-6)

This piece for solo piano showcases Chopin's mastery of grand melodic development in an extended *sonata* form. After an initial statement of melody, the composer puts the motif through a long string of continuous, elegant variations. Written near the end of his life, this elegant Barcarolle shows Chopin's piano style at its most highly developed.

Other Recommended Works: Preludes; op. 28; Waltzes; Mazurkas; Polonaises

Felix Mendelssohn (1809 - 1847)

Emerging as an exceptional child prodigy, Mendelssohn composed some of his most enduring music before the age of 20. His elegant and charming music was more conservative than innovative, reflecting a conscious restraint and gentility of the earlier classical era.

Midsummer Night's Dream, Overture (1826)

Mendelssohn wrote this impressive overture to Shakespeare's *A Midsummer Night's Dream* at age 17. The spirited and unrelenting use of the strings inspires a sense of the play's nocturnal magic, and this *incidental music* takes on a mystical life of its own.

Other Recommended Works: Symphony No. 3; Symphony No. 4; Trio for piano, violin, and cello

Hector Berlioz (1803 - 1869)

An eccentric and unpredictable Frenchman working in Paris, Berlioz earned his living as a music critic, conductor, and composer. Berlioz had little real acceptance in Paris, partly because he made enemies with his unusually truthful newspaper articles; and partly because his music was played badly there. He had a great following in Germany, England, and Russia.

Symphonie Fantastique, Op. 14, 2nd mvt. (1830)

Berlioz's *Symphonie Fantastique* is one of the first major works of ***programme music*** (music illustrating a non-musical idea). Much of the tremendous influence of programme music stems from this composition. In this case, the piece describes a miserable young poet enmeshed in a failed love. This second movement is a waltz scene where the poet's lover appears unexpectedly and then vanishes into a swirling crowd. Listen for a strange theme, seeming to have nothing to do with the rest of the composition – that's the woman, emerging from the waltzing crowd.

Other Recommended Works: Requiem; Romeo and Juliet

Johannes Brahms (1833 - 1897)

Brahms represents the highest level of music by the so-called "classical romanticists" – later 19th century composers who drew upon the past rather than striving for "originality." The musically conservative Brahms and his rival Richard Wagner (of *Ring Cycle* fame) disagreed on whether composers should endeavor to be truly "new" (Wagner) or keep traditions alive through connection to the past (Brahms).

Variations in B flat major on a theme by Haydn, Op. 56a "St. Anthony", Theme and Variations 1, 2 and 3 (1873)

This full Theme and Variations consists of an opening melody (originally used by Haydn) followed by eight variations and a large concluding movement. Brahms' work in the theme and variation medium was considered old-fashioned, but he showed that the form still had a long life ahead of it.

Other Recommended Works: Symphonies 1-4; A German Requiem; Piano Quartet No. 2

John Philip Sousa (1854 - 1932)

Though not usually considered a classical composer, John Philip Sousa elevated the march to high art in the late 19th century and his masterworks continue to dominate the form today. The tour of Sousa's Band in Europe in 1900 to 1905 ignited a European passion for American popular music.

March, Semper Fidelis (1888)

Listen closely to this piece and you'll hear your foot stamping. Drums start rolling. Horns start blaring. How can anyone resist a good march? This straightforward military parade tune shows how the king of American march music created a "classical popular" medium. Semper Fidelis (meaning "Always Faithful") was adopted by the United States Marines as its official march music.

Other Recommended Works: Any March, especially Stars and Stripes Forever and Washington Post

EARLY 20TH CENTURY

Unlike previous periods, the shift in music at the beginning of the 20th century was caused by a fundamental shift in society as much as any innovation in the music itself.

Music changed at this moment in history to mirror the dramatic changes taking place in the world around the composers. The composers' voices were saying: "The music of previous eras is nice, but it doesn't represent our time. We are surrounded by airplanes, Einstein's relativity, World Wars, Freud's psychology, and mass production. Baroque, Classic and Romantic styles don't represent the world we see around us."

The result? Listen for yourself to the musical representations of airplanes, Einstein, Freud and World Wars in Copland, Stravinsky, Ives and Bartok on CD No. 2. As you do, consider that when Beethoven wrote the 'Eroica' Symphony (Track 1 of CD 2) critics screeched: "What is this new music? This dissonance is horrible!". Some 200 years later, it is obvious even to lay listeners that their ear muscles merely needed a little training to appreciate the new sounds.

Significant Composers not included: Berg, Crawford Seeger, Debussy, Hindemith, Mahler, Milhaud, Ravel, Schoenberg, Shostakovich and Webern.

Aaron Copland (1900 - 1990)

Often referred to as "the Dean of American music," Copland wrote towering classics for the concert and ballet stages. His distinctively rhythmic style is based on American country dancing and evokes a purely American sound. Copland worked tirelessly to foster the careers of other composers. This work continues even today, well after his death, as he left most of his estate to a foundation (The Aaron Copland Fund for Music) which supports new-music activity in the New York area.

Fanfare for the Common Man (1942)

This short, powerful piece presents the essential Copland style in a three-minute curtain raiser. The interplay of regal hornplay and aggressive *tympani* shows a stylistic debt to the Stravinsky primal rhythms.

Other Recommended Works: Appalachian Spring; Rodeo (ballet scores)

Igor Stravinsky (1882 - 1971)

Generally associated with the 20th century's avant-garde and modernist movements, Russian-born Igor Stravinsky is a musical icon of his time and one of the most powerful compositional personalities of the last 100 years. Stravinsky's works are immediately recognizable by his sense of unexpected rhythm, dissonant harmonic style and unprecedented use of orchestral color.

Le sacre du printemps, "Danse Sacrale" (a.k.a. The Rite of Spring, last mvt.) (1913)

Widely considered Stravinsky's signature piece, *The Rite of Spring* was originally written as a score to accompany the choreography of ballet virtuoso Vaslav Nijinsky. The premiere of The *Rite of Spring* in 1913 was met by rioting, which was often cited by Stravinsky's enemies to illustrate how offensive his music was (both literally and figuratively). It is believed now that the rioting resulted from a disjointed performance. A concert performance (music only, no dance) of The Rite of Spring not long afterwards made Stravinsky an international celebrity.

Other Recommended Works: Petrouchka; Symphony of Psalms; Agon (ballet)

Charles Ives (1874 - 1954)

Ignored for most of his lifetime, Charles Ives was the most astonishingly original composer of the last century. Ives' music is astounding for its emotional range, incredible complexity, and its close bond with everyday American genres (ragtime, military marches, church music and popular songs). He wrote some 150 songs, whose unorthodox style and intensely dramatic content transformed American song.

Three Places in New England, mvt. 2, "Putnam's Camp" (1914)

In Putnam's Camp, Ives describes an imaginary scene, where a little boy falls asleep in the middle of a camp ground and dreams that groups of Revolutionary War soldiers are returning to the camp from different directions, each preceded by a marching band. The groups are marching to different tunes, and at different speeds, and the musical chaos gets more and more intense until they collide in the middle of the camp. It brings perspective to know that Charles Ives grew up watching his father conduct marching band contests. Similar to the setting in Putnam's Camp, his father would have the bands march into one another, playing different tunes, and the band that held together most in tact through the chaos would win.

Béla Bartók (1881 - 1945)

Fleeing Nazism to obscurity in New York City, Bartok pursued a vital contemporary composing style that would marry Bach's skillful counter-point, Beethoven's clarity and boldness, and Debussy's orchestral coloring. This Hungarian composer made his place in history through his ground-breaking fusion of East European folk music with the most rigorous classical background.

Concerto for Orchestra, mvt. 4 (1943)

Written near the end of his life, this concerto is considered one of Bartok's greatest pieces and one of the most exciting symphonic pieces of the century. Lively, intertwining melodies fluidly connect short instrumental solos as unpredictable rhythm and dynamic directions keep the listener enchanted.

Other Recommended Works: Piano Concertos 1-3; Music for String, Percussion, and Celesta; String Quartet No. 4

LATE 20TH CENTURY AND BEYOND

The best works of today are equally as accomplished as any in the past. Since the time of Beethoven, however, there has been a delay between the contemporary classical composer and the emergence of the audience he or she ultimately reaches. As this process takes place over the next 50 to 100 years for today's composers, the works and names of these composers will stake their place in history.

Rather than waiting 100 years for history to be chronicled, we believe these works and composers are worthy of discovery today. So Blue Marble Music's next volume in the Classical Explorer Series will be an exploration of contemporary composers and their works.

For your own advance exploration and knowledge, the following composers (all now over the age of 60) have had distinguished careers and have been considered the upper echelon of classical music since 1945. Most are alive today and are currently receiving commissions and performances with major orchestras and opera companies.

Adams, John – America
Babbitt, Milton – America
Berio, Luciano – Italy
Boulez, Pierre – France
Britten, Benjamin – England
Carter, Elliott – America
Crumb, George – America
Gubaidulina, Sofia – Russia
Harbison, John – America
Henze, Hans Werner – Germany

Ligeti, György – Transylvania
Lutoslawski, Witold – Poland
Messiaen, Olivier – France
Pärt, Arvo – Estonia
Schuller, Gunther – America
Schnittke, Alfred – Russia
Shostakovich, Dmitry – Russia
Stockhausen, Karlheinz – Germany
Takemitsu, Toru – Japan
Tippett, Michael – England
Tower, Joan – America

WHERE TO HEAR THEM

We are lucky. Almost any large city now has a good symphony and some have good opera houses. If you happen to be in the vicinity of any of the following groups in the U.S., we highly recommend attending a performance.

Atlanta Symphony Orchestra
Boston Symphony Orchestra
Chicago Lyric Opera
Chicago Symphony Orchestra
Cleveland Orchestra
Dallas Symphony
Houston Grand Opera
Los Angeles Philharmonic
Metropolitan Opera (New York)

National Symphony Orchestra (D.C.)
New York City Opera
New York Philharmonic
Philadelphia Orchestra
San Francisco Symphony
Sante Fe Opera
Seattle Symphony
St. Louis Symphony

GLOSSARY OF TERMS

Accompaniment – instrumental and/or vocal music that functions as the musical 'background' to a 'foreground' such as a melody.

Cantata – Usually, a Baroque-era composition for voice(s) and instruments, resembling a miniature opera (when secular) or oratorio (when sacred).

Chord – The sound made by three or more notes played at the same time. (e.g.: C-E-G on the piano). See also Scale.

Concerto – A piece of music that features the virtuosity of one or more players, the "soloist(s)", accompanied by an orchestra. The soloist and the orchestra often engage in a kind of musical conversation.

Consonance – A simultaneous sounding of tones producing an effect of complete blending. See also Dissonance.

Dissonance – A simultaneous sounding of tones that seems unblended, producing a feeling of tension or unrest and prompting movement toward a more relaxed sound (the "resolution") that will resolve the tension.

Counterpoint – Music consisting of two or more melodies sounding simultaneously. The word comes from the idea of setting every point in each melody against points in the others. More or less synonymous with polyphony.

Flat – A notational sign indicating that a given pitch is to be performed one half-step lower. (a half-step is the distance between any two immediately adjacent keys on the piano). See also Sharp.

Harmony – The simultaneous sounding of several notes. This could be said to be synonymous with the word chord, but in practice harmony implies a much wider-ranging set of musical associations and practices than chord.

Key – In Western music, especially from the 17th to the late 19th century, each piece usually seems to be oriented around a single pitch which also is the central pitch of the final sound of the piece. Such music is said to be in a "key". See also Pitch.

Imitation or Imitative Layering – Creating unity in a polyphonic piece by having a short piece of melody repeated by each of the various voices in succession. The technique is also called melodic layering. See also Counterpoint.

Incidental Music – Music performed during the action of a spoken play, including overtures and interludes.

Mass – The central service of the Roman Catholic Church. The importance of the mass prompted composers in every era to set its text to music.

Melody – A succession of singular pitches that seems to have complete coherence.

Meter – The sense that a piece of music has a pulse or beat, most often in patterns of two, three or four. When we tap our feet or move our bodies to music, we are feeling the meter. See also Rhythm.

Monophonic – Music consisting of only one melody with no accompaniment.

Motet – A vocal composition with a sacred text, most often in Latin and without accompaniment (a cappella).

Movement – Large compositions are often subdivided into separate sections that are self-contained. These sections are called movements and are normally played at different speeds.

GLOSSARY OF TERMS

Opera – A complete play set to music and normally performed in costume and with scenery. "Opera" means "work", and the term is a short form of "dramatic work set to music".

Opus – Literally "work" (the plural in Latin is "opera"). All the works of a composer often bear 'opus numbers' which signify the chronological order in which they were published.

Oratorio – A large-scale composition using a sacred text taken from, or based on, the Bible.

Orchestra – a performing ensemble that usually has about 20 to 110 instrumentalists.

Pitch – Our mental interpretation of the rate of vibration of the sound produced by a voice or instrument. Sounds that vibrate quickly are called high pitches; those that vibrate slowly are called low pitches.

Polyphony – Music in which two or more melodies sound simultaneously. See also Counterpoint.

Program Music – Instrumental music composed to have a powerful connection with a non-musical idea such as an essay, a painting or a story.

Rhythm – Anything having to do with the organization of time in music. Rhythm may be patterned, free, chaotic, or any mixture. The term is often confused with meter. See also Meter.

Scale – The basic pitch material of music, usually arranged in a simple order of ascending pitches. There are vast numbers of these in the world's music. The basic ones in classical music, from the 17th century on, are major and minor. Pieces written in "major keys" are often described as more cheerful than those in "minor keys". See also Key.

Sacred – Pertaining to religious worship.

Secular – Pertaining to everyday life, rather than religious worship.

Sharp – A notational sign indicating that the given pitch is to be performed one half-step higher. See also Flat.

Single Affect – Restricting a composition, or a movement of a composition, to communicating only a single emotion. Typical of Baroque music.

Sonata – A general term for instrumental works composed in multiple movements. The characteristics of sonatas are found in many works with other titles. For example, a symphony is really a sonata for full orchestra.

Suite – A piece consisting of several movements, normally based on popular dances.

Symphony – A work usually composed for a large orchestra, often in four movements. Also refers to the orchestra itself (i.e. Boston Symphony Orchestra).

Tempo – Refers to the speed at which a piece is performed. See also Rhythm and Meter.

Texture – A way of describing the sense that music is like a fabric – woven of melodies and harmonies.

Theme & Variations – A piece with a series of movements, the first of which is usually an easily remembered melody. This theme is then followed by a series of variations, each of which elaborates the theme differently, with changes in melody, harmony, rhythm, or texture.

Two-Voice Polarity – In a polyphonic piece, especially of the Baroque, the idea of concentrating the attention on both the melody and the bass, with everything in the middle acting as supporting filler.

RECOMMENDED RECORDINGS

cd 1

1. Composer: Anonymous
Title: Beloved Mother Of God (Beata Del Genitrix [Maria])
Performer: Choir Of The Monks Of
The Abbey of Montserrat
Label & #: ℗ 1974 Deutsche Grammophon, Universal
Timing: 2:25

2. Composer: Hildegard Von Bingen
Title: Antiphon: Studium Divinitatis
Performer: Anonymous 4 Ensemble
Label & #: ℗ 1997 Harmonia Mundi USA, HMU 907200
Timing: 1:12

3. Composer: Josquin DesPres
Title: Kyrie, from Missa L'homme arme sexti toni
Conductor: Peter Phillips
Performer: The Tallis Scholars
Label & #: ℗ 1989 Gimell Records, CDGIM 454919
Timing: 3:39

4. Composer: Giovanni Pierluigi da Palestrina
Title: Missa Papae Marcelli (Gloria)
Conductor: Peter Phillips
Performer: The Tallis Scholars
Label & #: ℗ 1989 Gimell Records, CDGIM 339
Timing: 5:28

5. Composer: Giovanni Gabrieli
Title: Canzon Septimi Toni No. 2
Performer: Philadelphia Brass Ensemble &
Cleveland Brass Ensemble
Label & #: ℗ Sony Music Entertainment Inc., MHK 62353
Timing: 2:48

6. Composer: Claudio Monteverdi
Title: Fourth Book Of Madrigals: A un giro sol de begl'occhi
Conductor: Anthony Rooley
Performer: Consort of Musike
Label & #: ℗ 1986 Decca Music Group Limited, Decca #
414 148-2
Timing: 2:12

7. Composer: Heinrich Schutz
Title: Die Himmel erzahlen Die Ehre Gottes, SWV 386
Conductor: Craig Smith
Performer: The Chorus of Emmanuel Music
Label & #: ℗ Koch International # 3-7174-2 H1
Timing: 5:09

8. Composer: George Frideric Handel
Title: Hallelujah (no. 39 from the Messiah)
Conductor: Neville Marriner
Performer: Academy of St. Martin in the Fields
Label & #: ℗ Philips Classics, Decca,
Universal, PH 4347723
Timing: 3:41

9. Composer: Johann Sebastian Bach
Title: Air On the G String
(from Suite no. 3 in D, BWV 1068)
Conductor: Neville Marriner
Performer: Academy of St.-Martin-In-the-Fields
Label & #: ℗ Philips Classics,
Decca, Universal, 2PH2 446533
Timing: 7:11

10. Composer: Johann Sebastian Bach
Title: Christmas Oratorio, BWV 248, Triumph, Rejoicing
Conductor: Karl Muenchinger
Performer: Stuttgart Chamber Orchestra
Label & #: ℗ 1967 Decca Music Group Limited,
2LC10 455783
Timing: 7:41

11. Composer: Joseph Haydn
Title: Symphony No. 103 in E flat,
Finale – Allegro Con Spirito
Conductor: Frans Brüggen
Performer: Orchestra of the 18th Century
Label & #: ℗ Philips Classics,
Decca, Universal, 028944278828
Timing: 5:24

12. Composer: Wolfgang Amadeus Mozart
Title: Don Giovanni, Duettino (no. 7),
La ci darem la mano
Conductor: Sir Colin Davis
Performer: Orchestra Of The Royal Opera House
Covent Garden; Ingvar Wixell, Arroyo, Martina,
Dame, Kiri Te Kanawa
Label & #: ℗ Philips Classics,
Decca, Universal, 3PME 422541
Timing: 3:40

13. Composer: Wolfgang Amadeus Mozart
Title: Die Zauberflote "The Magic Flute," K. 620, Overture
Conductor: Hans Vonk
Performer: Staatskapelle Dresden
Label & #: ℗ 1990 Delta Entertainment, Laserlight 15885
Timing: 7:08

14. Composer: Wolfgang Amadeus Mozart
Title: Piano Concerto No. 23 in A
Conductor: Alfred Wallenstein
Performer: Artur Rubinstein,
RCA Victor Symphony Orchestra
Label & #: ℗ RCA Victor, BMG, 63061
Timing: 7:20

1. Composer: Ludwig van Beethoven
Title: Symphony no. 3 in E flat major, Op. 55,
Allegro con brio
Conductor: Sir Georg Solti
Performer: Chicago Symphony Orchestra
Label & #: ℗ Decca Music, Universal, 2LH6 430400
Timing: 17:55

2. Composer: Frédéric Chopin
Title: Barcarolle for Piano in F# major (Op. 60)
Performer: Martha Argerich
Label & #: ℗ Deutsche Grammophon,
Universal, 2GOR 447430
Timing: 8:07

3. Composer: Feliz Mendelssohn
Title: A Midsummer Night's Dream, Op. 21, Overture
Conductor: Seiji Ozawa
Performer: Boston Symphony Orchestra
Label & #: ℗ Deutsche Grammophon,
Universal, 2GH 439897
Timing: 6:15

4. Composer: Hector Berlioz
Title: Symphonie Fantastique, Op. 14, Allegro non troppo
Conductor: Sir Colin Davis
Performer: The Royal Concertgebouw Orchestra
Label & #: ℗ Philips Classics,
Decca, Universal, 2PH 411425
Timing: 6:14

5. Composer: Johannes Brahms
Title: Variations in B flat major on a theme by Haydn,
Op. 56a (excerpt)
Conductor: Bernard Haitink
Performer: Boston Symphony Orchestra
Label & #: ℗ Philips Classics, Universal, 456030
Timing: 6:20

6. Composer: John Philip Sousa
Title: Semper Fidelis (March)
Conductor: Lt. Col. F.J. Harris
Performer: The Band of the Grenadier Guards
Label & #: ℗ Decca, Universal, 2LC 430211
Timing: 2:32

7. Composer: Aaron Copland
Title: Fanfare For The Common Man
Conductor: Zubin Mehta
Performer: Los Angeles Philharmonic Orchestra
Label & #: ℗ Decca, Universal
Timing: 2:47

8. Composer: Igor Stravinsky
Title: Le Sacre du Printemps (The Rite of Spring),
Last movement "Danse Sacrale"
Conductor: Igor Stravinsky
Label & #: ℗ Sony Music

9. Composer: Charles Ives
Title: Three Places In New England – Putnam's Camp
Conductor: Howard Hanson
Performer: Eastman Rochester Orchestra
Label & #: ℗ Mercury International
Timing: 5:40

10. Composer: Bela Bartok
Title: Concerto for Orchestra, Sz 116
Conductor: Antal Dorati
Performer: London Symphony Orchestra
Label & #: ℗ Philips Classics,
Decca, Universal, 2MM 432017
Timing: 9:36

CREDITS

PHOTOS AND ILLUSTRATIONS:

Cover Tsutomu Takasaki / Photonica

1, 3, 13, 22 and 19. Scala / Art Resource, NY

4. Tate Gallery, London / Art Resource, NY

6. Alinari / Art Resource, NY

9. Nan Melville

12 and 37. Giraudon / Art Resource, NY

15. Nimatallah / Art Resource, NY

17, 23, 26, 31, 32, 36, 40, 41 and 42. Erich Lessing / Art Resource, NY

25. PD Images

29. Illustration from Beaumarchais's *The Marriage of Figaro* (Paris, 1785)

38. Réunion de Musées Nationaux / Art Resource, NY

43 and 48. National Portrait Gallery, Smithsonian Institution / Art Resource, NY

46, 47, 49. Hulton Archive/Getty Images

51. Keith Goldstein / Photonica

Music Selection: John Heiss and Joel Sachs

Concept and Production Assistance: Derek Geary

Editors: Pableaux Johnson, Jane Tanner and Karol Stone

Music Licensing and Manufacturing: Universal Music Group

PRODUCED BY: STEVE STONE   DESIGN: GILES DESIGN INC.